Galatians in-depth study guide

By grace through faith

<u>Introduction</u>

Galatians In-Depth Bible Study

By grace through faith

Thank you so much for reading this book. I understand that there are other study guides available, so I really do appreciate you taking the time to read mine. As for this book, I give all the glory to God. Without Him, this wouldn't be possible.

You may notice that some passages were skipped, this is because I did not feel it on my heart to touch base on them. Therefore, there will be some gaps.

Throughout this study, when I refer to the enemy, I always use a lowercase letter, even if it's the first word in the sentence. I know that it may sound odd, considering we are taught not to do this, but this was intentional. So often we give the enemy power in our lives. Through anxiety, fear, depression, or whatever else it is that you you may be going through. I wanted to show you that he has no hold on a child of God. So when you see these "grammar issues", know that they were done on purpose. Use them as a reminder that satan has no hold on you. In the name of Jesus, you don't belong to him. You are God's, and God's alone.

To all who are reading this

Grace to you and peace from God the Father and our Lord Jesus Christ, who gave Himself for our sins, that He might deliver us from this present evil age, according to the will of our God and Father, to whom be glory forever and ever. Amen.

Galatians 1:3-5

Galatians 1:6-9

Don't be so quick to be led astray from the truth. Some preach other gospels, and they are not from, or of God. These people only want to trouble you and pervert the word of our Lord and Savior Jesus Christ. Do not listen to them. Even if an angel comes to you, preaching a different gospel than one according to the truth, do not listen! Turn your ear away and walk only in a manner worthy of Christ. Let those who lead you away be accursed.

Galatians 1:10

We seek not the pleasure of man, but of God. What we do, we do for Christ. Whether we are reviled, let it be so, whether we are mocked, let us be mocked, whatever it may be, count it all as loss, for the glory of our God.

If I spoke to please men, would I be a servant of the Lord? If I spoke to please men, would I speak against the things of this world? If I spoke to please men, would I speak of the things you don't want to hear? No, I tell you this, I speak to please God, and God alone.

Galatians 1:11-12

The gospel that we preach and speak of, is not of this world. We were not taught by man, but God.

Paul's encounter on Damascus road, led him to Jesus. Man had nothing to do with his coming to Jesus, nor did human words, but the words of God Himself. When we read the word, it is not man's words, but the word of God. God may have used others to write the bible, but it was the Holy Spirit that inspired them to do so. When you were led to Christ, someone may have led you there, but ultimately, it was the Holy Spirit working through that person, who actually led you to Christ. That person may have been the willing body, but it was ultimately the Holy Spirit who spoke to your heart and theirs. This reminds us that whatever we do in life, we must remember the true source of our being. The true source of our strength and courage, boldness and perseverance, is none other than God. Yes, others may strengthen us, but it is ultimately God who used that person to strengthen you. I say this in hopes that you will always remember who the true source of all that you have is. The true source has always been God, whether you have realized it or not.

For prophecy never had its origin in the human will, but prophets, though human, spoke from God as they were carried along by the Holy Spirit.

2 Peter 1:21

All Scripture is given by inspiration of God, and is profitable for doctrine, for reproof, for correction, for instruction in righteousness, that the man of God may be complete, thoroughly equipped for every good work.

2 Timothy 3:16-17

You see, there are times when we so easily forget, that God is the one guiding us. Yes, He may use others to help us along the way, but the guiding ultimately comes from God. You may plan your steps, but it is the Lord who establishes them.

In their hearts humans plan their course,
but the LORD establishes their steps.

Proverbs 16:9

A person's steps are directed by the LORD.
How then can anyone understand their own way?

Proverbs 20:24

Galatians 1:13-16

Paul's testimony goes to show you that God can use anyone. Paul, who once persecuted Christians, was now preaching the same gospel that he once persecuted. God used Paul as His instrument, regardless of his past, and this pleased God to do so. God was gracious in revealing His Son to Paul. He did not deserve it, but nonetheless, God used Him. This goes to show you, that your past does not define who you are. Your past does not make any difference in whether or not God is willing to use you, as we see God using Paul, who had a past that was far from perfect.

Galatians 1:16

I feel the need to ask you this question. Here we see that Paul's first instinct, was not to discuss this with flesh and blood. This leads me to ask the question, what is your first reaction when you need help, want to share news, or are unsure of something? Although God does use others to speak to you, the first person you should ask, is God.

Asking others for help is not wrong, but it's who you ask first that matters.

The way of fools seems right to them,
but the wise listen to advice.

Proverbs 12:15

Listen to advice and accept discipline,
and at the end you will be counted among the wise.

Proverbs 19:20

So you can see, it's not wrong to ask or accept advice, and it's not wrong to ask for help, but even then, you should still ask God to show you the right person to ask, and let you only hear sound advice.

As humans, we have a tendency to go to the wrong sources for advice. So after you have prayed about it, before you go to someone for advice, look at their life. Do they follow the Lord? Do they read? Do they pray? If you go to someone who says that they believe, but they clearly don't live a life for the Lord, then that may not be the best person to ask for advice. Only God can impress on your heart, who the right person to go to for advice is. All you need to do is ask, and believe. He does hear you. Remember, you have to make sure that who you are asking, will not give the advice of the world, but of God. Whenever something in your life arises, go to God first. Even if you plan on talking to someone else, still, go to God first. Ask God to only allow you to hear sound advice, and ask God to speak through that person to give you sound advice. Either way, the pattern is, go to God first.

Galatians 1:23-24

If you see a man, who previously denied the faith, cast his vote against Christians, and not follow Jesus, if you see this man now following Christ, you would have to come to no other conclusion other than giving the glory to God. A man who was so passionate about persecuting the church, and following the traditions of his fathers, now a changed man and following Christ. What other explanation is there? To change the heart of a man so set in his ways, takes more than mere coincidence. Therefore, God is the one who received the glory when they saw Paul, now a changed man, a new creation following Christ.

Galatians 1:23

These people didn't know Paul, yet they glorified God. They did this just by hearing about his testimony. This goes to show you that God can use your testimony in mighty ways, if you are willing. We gain strength from the testimony of others, we gain faith, gratitude, endurance, and so much more. When we read the testimonies in the bible, we are strengthened, encouraged, among many other things. They teach us so much, some which are patience, prayer even in difficult times, love, forgiveness, etc. Our testimony was not meant to go to the grave with us. I understand that some things are personal, but I am sure that there is something in your life that you are willing to share, that can encourage others. Even something like God answering your prayer about a job, a marriage, an addiction, or something else. It can be something that you think is too small to share, that could help and encourage the multitude. Don't let the enemy dumb down your testimony, because God can and will use it, if you let Him.

Galatians 2:2

Here we see that Paul went up by revelation. This means that not only did God tell Paul to go, but Paul listened.

What is it in your life that God has asked you to do, that you still have not done? Maybe it's something you don't feel capable of doing. The answer to this is, you don't need to be capable, because God is. Maybe God told you to be still, and you are getting ready to move ahead, because you are being impatient and don't want to wait. Maybe weeks, months, or years have passed, and you are tired of hearing wait. I know that feeling all too well, and I can assure you that moving without God's blessing, is NEVER a good option. As a matter of fact, it should never even be an option in your eyes. Why? Because even though it's hard to wait, God has something even better in mind for you than you could ever think, dream, or imagine. And in the meantime, God is building your endurance, faith, patience, character, perseverance, etc. DO NOT MOVE AHEAD IF GOD SAYS TO WAIT.

The point that I am trying to make is, are you doing what God has asked you to do? Every excuse that you could ever make as to why you haven't done what He has asked yet, is nothing but an excuse. It's a ploy that the enemy used to keep you exactly where you are, stagnant. The enemy wants you to do the exact opposite of what God asks. If God says stay, the enemy says go. If God says do this, the enemy says you can't. It's like the battle between Spirit and Flesh. They are always at odds because they can never agree on anything. You have to make the choice. Either you follow God, or you don't. You can't have both. You can't go in two directions at once, or you will be torn in half. So make the choice, who are you going to follow? And before you answer, remember,

You are of God, little children, and have overcome them, because He who is in you is greater than he who is in the world.

1 John 4:4

I can do all things through Christ who strengthens me.

Philippians 4:13

I also want to add that this scripture above in Philippians, is not as black and white as it may seem. I say this, because if you look at the context, it's not saying that you can do anything and everything. It's saying that no matter what it is you face, whether good or bad, you can get through it, because it is Christ who gives you strength. Some people look at this and say I can do anything, because Christ strengthens me, but the real meaning is, that you can get through anything because it is Christ who strengthens you. Here is some more context from the NIV to give you a bit of a better understanding.

I am not saying this because I am in need, for I have learned to be content whatever the circumstances. I know what it is to be in need, and I know what it is to have plenty. I have learned the secret of being content in any and every situation, whether well fed or hungry, whether living in plenty or in want. I can do all this through him who gives me strength.

Philippians 4:11-13

This means that no matter what you go through, you can get through it. So using this scripture towards doing what God asks of you, is not saying that it's smooth sailing. It's saying that if you choose to do what God has asked of you, then it may be difficult, but you can endure it, and get through it, because of He who gives you the strength to. And yes, sometimes you may get things wrong. Sometimes you may think that God wants you to do something, and you get it wrong. Guess what? That's OK, because God knows your heart, and He knows that you are trying to please Him. This is all part of the process of growing up in spiritual maturity. Meaning that falling down is all part of getting to know God's voice. How do you get to know someone's voice? You spend time with them, and you listen to them. Sometimes that includes some trial and error, but don't be afraid to step out, just because you are afraid to get things wrong. Because then you are doing exactly what you didn't want to do in the first place, not listening to God. It's better to try and fail, than never to try at all. Trying means that you may get some things right, and you may get some things wrong, but not trying at all, is 100% not getting anything right, and not listening to God at all. Trying means that you are walking by faith, and not by sight. Trying, is putting the effort to do as God asks, sitting stagnant, is not.

<u>Galatians 2:3-5</u>

This is a perfect example of wolves among sheep. Ones who claim to be for God, but are really against God. They sought to remove the freedom that they had been given through Christ. These wolves preferred them to be in bondage, but, they did not succeed in their attempts to mislead them. They did not submit to their lies, even for a moment. They wanted the truth to remain in them, and they wanted only to speak of what is true. So they guarded themselves, and continued in the truth.

This is why it's so important to guard yourself. Some claim to be your friends, or those there to help you, but they are wolves among sheep. There can be wolves in church, as well as everyday life, so be careful. Pray and ask God for discernment to be able to tell the wolves from the sheep, lest they lead you astray.

Galatians 2:6

Just because someone seems to be something, means nothing. If a speaker has a billion followers, this means nothing. They are not favored more by God in any way, and they are not loved more, as God shows no favoritism. Too many people put their focus on the person doing the speaking, instead of the One speaking through them. We are but a vessel. We are used by God, and the glory is always God's, never ours. Instead of looking at someone speaking, and caring about how big their platform is, remember the One who allowed that platform to come into existence. Whatever they have, was gifted to them by God. They were but a willing vessel. A servant doing what their Master has asked of them, does not deserve the glory for what the Master built through them. This is not to say that you don't uplift them and tell them that they did a good job, because you should, but be careful who you make your idol. There is only One who should be your focus. That's God, and God alone. Not a mere human being, but God Himself.

Galatians 2:7-9

The same God who worked through Peter, also worked through Paul. Here he acknowledges that it is not of himself that he was committed to teaching the Gentiles, but the authority to do so, came from God.

I want to emphasize on the fact that we should always give the glory to God. The glory is never ours to have. Don't be like the nine lepers, who did not return to give God the glory, after they were healed.

Now it happened as He went to Jerusalem that He passed through the midst of Samaria and Galilee. Then as He entered a certain village, there met Him ten men who were lepers, who stood afar off. And they lifted up their voices and said, "Jesus, Master, have mercy on us!"

So when He saw them, He said to them, "Go, show yourselves to the priests." And so it was that as they went, they were cleansed.

And one of them, when he saw that he was healed, returned, and with a loud voice glorified God, and fell down on his face at His feet, giving Him thanks. And he was a Samaritan.

So Jesus answered and said, "Were there not ten cleansed? But where are the nine? Were there not any found who returned to give glory to God except this foreigner?" And He said to him, "Arise, go your way. Your faith has made you well."

Luke 17:11-19

Galatians 2:11-14

Peter had allowed the multitude to affect his clarity. Peter knew what was right, but he still refused the truth. He did this because the people of the circumcision, denied the truth. The truth is that the Gentiles now have the same inheritance as the Jews. Peter used to eat with these Gentiles, but he was swayed by the crowd, and when they came, he would not eat with them. Therefore, Peter separated himself from the Gentiles, because he looked more for the recognition of man, than God. Paul however, called out Peter in front of all.

Those who are sinning rebuke in the presence of all, that the rest also may fear.

1 Timothy 5:20

Do not allow yourself to be influenced by the multitude. Do not blend in with the world, rather, stand out. Remember, we do not seek the approval of man, but God. We do not seek to be accepted by man, but God. If a crowd rejects you for your faith, then so be it. If a crowd mocks you for believing, then so be it. It may feel bad to be denied and rejected by man, but much worse to be rejected by God. Therefore, live for Jesus, not man, because you will one day face Jesus Christ, and I would much rather have an eternity of open arms from Jesus, than the temporary praise of man.

Galatians 2:14

Here we see that the rest of the Jews, and even Barnabas, were carried away with these lies, these false beliefs. Once one believes a lie, it's much easier for the rest to believe. Therefore, we must be careful not to be carried away by false teachings, as it will not only affect us, but also those around us.

Galatians 2:16

A man is not saved by his works, but by faith in Jesus Christ. This is the only name in which you can be saved. Some believe that good works will get you into heaven, however, this is false.

For by grace you have been saved through faith, and that not of yourselves; it is the gift of God, not of works, lest anyone should boast. For we are His workmanship, created in Christ Jesus for good works, which God prepared beforehand that we should walk in them.

Ephesians 2:8-10

If you were saved by your own works, perhaps you would be boastful of the things that you have done. We are not saved from works, because it is God who gets the glory, not us. You were saved by grace, through faith, lest anyone should boast. Instead, we put away boastful talk, and we boast in the one who deserves all the glory for our salvation, Jesus Christ.

for by the works of the law no flesh shall be justified.

Galatians 2:16

This scripture above, shows that no one will be justified by their works. If you don't believe in Jesus, and you think that your works will get you into heaven, then I pray that your eyes may be opened right now in the name of Jesus Christ. I pray that you see this truth that is right in front of your eyes. The truth is that your only entry into heaven, is through Jesus Christ. He is the door, and all others are thieves and robbers.

"Most assuredly, I say to you, he who does not enter the sheepfold by the door, but climbs up some other way, the same is a thief and a robber. But he who enters by the door is the shepherd of the sheep. To him the doorkeeper opens, and the sheep hear his voice; and he calls his own sheep by name and leads them out. And when he brings out his own sheep, he goes before them; and the sheep follow him, for they know his voice. Yet they will by no means follow a stranger, but will flee from him, for they do not know the voice of strangers." Jesus used this illustration, but they did not understand the things which He spoke to them.

Then Jesus said to them again, "Most assuredly, I say to you, I am the door of the sheep. All who ever came before Me are thieves and robbers, but the sheep did not hear them. I am the door. If anyone enters by Me, he will be saved, and will go in and out and find pasture. The thief does not come except to steal, and to kill, and to destroy. I have come that they may have life, and that they may have it more abundantly.

"I am the good shepherd. The good shepherd gives His life for the sheep. But a hireling, he who is not the shepherd, one who does not own the sheep, sees the wolf coming and leaves the sheep and flees; and the wolf catches the sheep and scatters them.

John 10:1-12

There is only One door that you can enter through, and that door is Jesus Christ.

But what does it say? "The word is near you, in your mouth and in your heart" (that is, the word of faith which we preach): that if you confess with your mouth the Lord Jesus and believe in your heart that God has raised Him from the dead, you will be saved. For with the heart one believes unto righteousness, and with the mouth confession is made unto salvation. For the Scripture says, "Whoever believes on Him will not be put to shame."

Romans 10:8-11

Galatians 2:17-19

When we were saved, we became a new creation. We stopped living for the world and its desires, and started living for Jesus. It's not God's fault, if I decide to once again build the things of this world inside of me. The things that were once destroyed when I believed, and choose to follow the path of Christ. We were given free will, so that choice falls on me, not God. Therefore, if I build again those things that I once destroyed, I make myself a transgressor. We made a choice, once we were saved, to live for God. We chose to follow Jesus Christ. When we chose this, we put on a new self.

That, however, is not the way of life you learned when you heard about Christ and were taught in him in accordance with the truth that is in Jesus. You were taught, with regard to your former way of life, to put off your old self, which is being corrupted by its deceitful desires; to be made new in the attitude of your minds; and to put on the new self, created to be like God in true righteousness and holiness.

Ephesians 4:20-24

When we put off our old self, we became a new creation, created in Christ Jesus.

Therefore, if anyone is in Christ, he is a new creation; old things have passed away; behold, all things have become new.

2 Corinthians 5:17

This means that your former conduct, your former desires of the flesh, and everything that is of this world, gets put away from you. You have now made the choice to live for Christ. When you did this, you were crucified with Christ, and it is now no longer you who lives, but Christ in you. Christ now dwells inside of you, and you are not your own. You belong to God, and you are His child. Therefore, you have chosen to now live a life of faith, through Jesus Christ, the son of God. The same Son who loves you so much, that He gave His life for you. I don't know about you, but for someone to love me so much, that they died for me, watches over me 24/7, loves me unconditionally, despite all of my faults, is faithful to us, even when we are not faithful to Him, has seated us with Him in the heavenly places, etc, this is someone that I want to follow. This is someone I want to live my life for. There is no one else I would rather serve.

Galatians 2:21

I do not set aside the gift of God, for if we were made righteous through the law, then what did Christ die for?

Galatians 3:1-4

Some start in the Spirit, and end in the flesh. One who is born again, follows Christ and faces many tribulations. They may start with fervency for the Lord, praising Him in Spirit and truth. These people have gone about suffering for the gospel, being persecuted, made fun of, and endure the narrow path. Some go through what you may call a honeymoon faze. In the beginning you may be fervent, seeking the Lord at all times. You may be willing to share with everyone you meet, the good news of Jesus Christ. But, somewhere along the way, you realize that this path is hard. Maybe you give up, maybe you decide to go your own way, or maybe you are led astray. These people have begun in the Spirit, but ended in the flesh. Things got tough so they bailed, their friends made fun of them, so they stopped following Christ, or maybe you just don't have the time anymore. This reminds me of the parable that Jesus explained in Matthew.

"Listen then to what the parable of the sower means: When anyone hears the message about the kingdom and does not understand it, the evil one comes and snatches away what was sown in their heart. This is the seed sown along the path. The seed falling on rocky ground refers to someone who hears the word and at once receives it with joy. But since they have no root, they last only a short time. When trouble or persecution comes because of the word, they quickly fall away. The seed falling among the thorns refers to someone who hears the word, but the worries of this life and the deceitfulness of wealth choke

the word, making it unfruitful. But the seed falling on good soil refers to someone who hears the word and understands it. This is the one who produces a crop, yielding a hundred, sixty or thirty times what was sown."

Matthew 13:18-23

Either way, these people have started in the Spirit, and ended in the flesh. When I was younger, I had so much fervency for the Lord. I prayed to Him, talked to Him, read the word, etc. As time went on and I grew older, I stopped reading. I prayed, but not like I used to. I started in the Spirit, but somewhere along the way, I ended in the flesh. Thankfully, God loves His children so much, that through His great mercy and grace, He brought me back to Him. What I am trying to say is, it's easy to lose focus on what truly matters, because life has a tendency to get in the way. Sometimes, you can get off track from the smallest thing, and it just spirals from there. The enemy knows what he is doing. I say this because he has been doing it for longer than you and I have been alive. The enemy knows what makes you tick, what makes you stray, what makes you lose focus, etc. I say that we take a stand. I say that we stop letting him take our focus away from Jesus. I say that we put our foot down, with satan underneath it, and push on with our race in God through Christ Jesus. Distractions are eminent, following those distractions, are not. As long as we are in these fleshly bodies, here on earth, we will face distraction after distraction. satan won't let up, and neither should we. Will you be willing, to take that stand with me?

Galatians 3:1-4

Your eyes knew Christ as crucified. You didn't just see with your eyes, but you saw with your heart. You didn't see through fleshly eyes, but spiritual ones. However, something has made you stray from this truth.

The Holy Spirit within you, was never given to you because of your works. It is by grace, through faith, that you were sealed with His promise. Do not foolishly walk about in the flesh, but adhere to a life lived through the Spirit. Do not let your sufferings, be in vain. Remember who you are in Christ, and walk accordingly.

Galatians 3:5-9

God's promises never cease to fail. God told Abraham that through him, all the nations would be blessed.

Then the Angel of the LORD called to Abraham a second time out of heaven, and said: "By Myself I have sworn, says the LORD, because you have done this thing, and have not withheld your son, your only son— blessing I will bless you, and multiplying I will multiply your descendants as the stars of the heaven and as the sand which is on the seashore; and your descendants shall possess the gate of their enemies. In your seed all the nations of the earth shall be blessed, because you have obeyed My voice."

Genesis 22:15-18

See also Genesis 12:1-4

God kept His promise, and justified the Gentiles by faith. We, who believe in our Lord Jesus's death and resurrection, are part of this promise. We are sons and daughters of Abraham. This promise was given to those who believe in Jesus, not because of what we have done, but through grace, by faith. It is a gift from God.

being justified freely by His grace through the redemption that is in Christ Jesus

Romans 3:24

For by grace you have been saved through faith, and that not of yourselves; it is the gift of God

Ephesians 2:8

Because Abraham believed God, it was accounted to him as righteousness. His faith, not his works. Therefore, only those of us who have faith, are sons of Abraham. We must have faith in God's Son, Jesus Christ. As we have read previously in this study, that it is only through Jesus Christ, that you will be saved.

<u>Galatians 3:10-12</u>

Have you ever been disrespectful to your parent? If you said yes, and you are of the works of the law, then you are cursed. In Deuteronomy we are told this.

'Cursed is the one who does not confirm all the words of this law by observing them.'

Deuteronomy 27:26

Please also see Deuteronomy 27 as a whole, to get more context.

This is why those who believe in Jesus Christ, are no longer of the works of the law, but faith. If we lived by the works of the law, we would be doomed to failure, as who could withhold them all?

For whoever keeps the whole law and yet stumbles at just one point is guilty of breaking all of it.

James 2:10

But please, do not think that this is abolishing the law by any means. On the contrary, we establish the law.

Do we then make void the law through faith? Certainly not! On the contrary, we establish the law.

Romans 3:31

The just shall live by faith. This does not mean that one should not follow the law. Those who have faith in Jesus Christ, want to obey God and follow His precepts, His laws. However, we are not justified by the law, but faith. A child obeys their parent because they respect them, also because they want to please them, and because they love them, this we should do also. This passage does not tell us that we shouldn't follow the teachings in the word of God, it is telling us that we are not justified by them. We do not have salvation through the law, nor do we have righteousness through it. If we did, then we would be saved by our works, and then what did Christ die for? Instead, we are saved by grace, through faith in Jesus Christ. This reminds me of a verse in Romans.

What shall we say then? Shall we continue in sin that grace may abound? Certainly not! How shall we who died to sin live any longer in it? Or do you not know that as many of us as were baptized into Christ Jesus were baptized into His death? Therefore we were buried with Him through baptism into death, that just as Christ was raised from the dead by the glory of the Father, even so we also should walk in newness of life.

For if we have been united together in the likeness of His death, certainly we also shall be in the likeness of His resurrection, knowing this, that our old man was crucified with Him, that the body of sin might be done away with, that we should no longer be slaves of sin.

Romans 6:1-6

Those who are saved, are made new, and how could we live in sin any longer? Were we made free from sin, to be held captive by it again? Of course not!

Stand fast therefore in the liberty by which Christ has made us free, and do not be entangled again with a yoke of bondage.

Galatians 5:1

When we were saved, we became born again. This means that we were made new, and it is no longer us who live, but Christ in us, and if Christ is in us, then why would we want to go about sinning and following the world?

Dear children, do not let anyone lead you astray. The one who does what is right is righteous, just as he is righteous. The one who does what is sinful is of the devil, because the devil has been sinning from the beginning. The reason the Son of God appeared was to destroy the devil's work. No one who is born of God will continue to sin, because God's seed remains in them; they cannot go on sinning, because they have been born of God. This is how we know who the children of God are and who the children of the devil are: Anyone who does not do what is

right is not God's child, nor is anyone who does not love
their brother and sister.

1 John 3:7-10

Now this doesn't mean that we won't be tempted to sin, because we are still in the flesh, but we no longer walk by the flesh, but the Spirit. Meaning that we now have the power to overcome the fleshly desires of this world.
Before you were in Christ, the Holy Spirit did not live inside of you, therefore, you had no power to overcome the flesh. Now, because you are a new creation in Christ, that power lives within you through the Holy Spirit. So if you have flesh, warring against the Spirit, which would be stronger?

You, dear children, are from God and have overcome
them, because the one who is in you is greater than the
one who is in the world.

1 John 4:4

Therefore, if you belong to Christ, then you have all the power inside of you to overcome this world, just as Jesus did. Jesus not only overcame the world, but He also gave us all that He has, through the Holy Spirit. If we have all that He has, than that power to overcome the enemy is within us, you just have to realize it. And trust me when I tell you, the enemy will try really hard to keep you from this truth. Why? Because once you realize the strength that you have within you, it's game over for the enemy. The enemy then loses his power over you, and you now have the chance to not only free yourself from his bondage, but also to free others, and of course, the enemy hates that. So the sooner you realize how much authority that you actually have over the enemy, the better.

However, when He, the Spirit of truth, has come, He will guide you into all truth; for He will not speak on His own authority, but whatever He hears He will speak; and He will tell you things to come. He will glorify Me, for He will take of what is Mine and declare it to you. All things that the Father has are Mine. Therefore I said that He will take of Mine and declare it to you.

John 16:13-15

Behold, I give you the authority to trample on serpents and scorpions, and over all the power of the enemy, and nothing shall by any means hurt you.

Luke 10:19

"I have told you these things, so that in me you may have peace. In this world you will have trouble. But take heart! I have overcome the world."

John 16:33

The fact of the matter is, you have to come to the realization that the enemy has literally zero hold on you. This is why we have a part to play. We see this in James.

Therefore submit to God. Resist the devil and he will flee from you.

James 4:7

This scripture doesn't just say that the devil will flee from you, but it specifically says that you have to resist the devil, and then he will flee from you. We have a part to play in his fleeing. That part is believing in the power that is within you, and truly believing that He who is in you is greater than he who is in the world. So what is your part in this? Submit to God, resist the devil, and believe that you have the power to overcome the enemy, and he will flee from you. You have to believe it, say it with authority, and don't just say it, but declare it, in the name of Jesus Christ. The devil has no hold over a child of God. The only One holding you, is God. Remember that.

Galatians 3:13-14

We were redeemed of that curse that we talked about previously, in the Galatians 3:10-12 study. How were we freed from this curse? We were freed because Jesus, in His great love and mercy, took on the debt that we owed. We were redeemed of our legal indebtedness. We owed much more than we could afford, and Jesus loves us so much, that He bore the shame for us. He was guiltless, yet took on our guilt. He was sinless, yet took on our sin. This was done for us, not because we deserved it, but because He loves us, immensely. He didn't have to do what He did, but He did it anyways, because that's how much He loves us. Because of this, we received the promise of the Spirit, through faith. How indescribable does someone have to be, to love us this much? I can name only One.

Galatians 3:13-14

I want to add that the old testament shows what people used to do. We used to make sacrifices for sins, because we are sinful people. We may not realize it, because it was so long ago, but Jesus put a stop to having to make those sacrifices, by being the final sacrifice needed for our sins. This is pretty powerful and amazing if you take a second to think about it. Imagine where we would be today, if not for Jesus. Before Jesus, sacrifices were made, Gentiles had no inheritance, etc. We need to realize that

God did so much for us, by Jesus's death on the cross. So much time has passed, that we have forgotten where we started. I for one, am extremely grateful that I have the opportunity, to be called a child of the Most High.

Therefore, just as sin entered the world through one man, and death through sin, and in this way death came to all people, because all sinned—

To be sure, sin was in the world before the law was given, but sin is not charged against anyone's account where there is no law. Nevertheless, death reigned from the time of Adam to the time of Moses, even over those who did not sin by breaking a command, as did Adam, who is a pattern of the one to come.

But the gift is not like the trespass. For if the many died by the trespass of the one man, how much more did God's grace and the gift that came by the grace of the one man, Jesus Christ, overflow to the many! Nor can the gift of God be compared with the result of one man's sin: The judgment followed one sin and brought condemnation, but the gift followed many trespasses and brought justification. For if, by the trespass of the one man, death reigned through that one man, how much more will those who receive God's abundant provision of grace and of the gift of righteousness reign in life through the one man, Jesus Christ!

Consequently, just as one trespass resulted in condemnation for all people, so also one righteous act resulted in justification and life for all people. For just as through the disobedience of the one man the many were made sinners, so also through the obedience of the one man the many will be made righteous.

Romans 5:12-19

Galatians 3:15-18

The seed of Abraham, is Jesus Christ. God gave this promise to Abraham, and no amount of time, can invalidate God's promise. When God makes a promise, He acts. It can not be undone by the amount of time that has passed. God is not a mere human, that He should change His mind.

God is not human, that he should lie,
not a human being, that he should change his mind.
Does he speak and then not act?
Does he promise and not fulfill?

Numbers 23:19

Galatians 3:18

Our inheritance is not of the law, but of the promise.

Galatians 3:26-29

I feel the need to point something out. God does not love men, more than women, and God does not love Jews, more than others. We are all equal in God's eyes. Gender, race, financial status, etc, do not affect God's love for you.

Some women may wonder why men were mentioned so much in the bible. You have to see that, woman were mentioned too, however, there is an order of things. For example, the order is that a woman should respect, and be submissive to her husband. He is the head of the household. This does not mean that God loves men more, it just means that there is an order of things.

Wives, submit yourselves to your own husbands as you do to the Lord. For the husband is the head of the wife as Christ is the head of the church, his body, of which he is the Savior. Now as the church submits to Christ, so also wives should submit to their husbands in everything.

Ephesians 5:22-33

Many of you may not like this, but this was God's design, not yours. We are in a society that says differently than what God says, therefore, passages like this, may make you question God's love for you, but don't. You are not loved any less than man. He made man with love, and He made you with that same love. Period.

You have to remember, that God made everything for its purpose, and there is an order in which things are created to be. If you see the passage after, we see that men have a part too.

Husbands, love your wives, just as Christ loved the church and gave himself up for her to make her holy, cleansing her by the washing with water through the word, and to present her to himself as a radiant church, without stain or wrinkle or any other blemish, but holy and blameless. In this same way, husbands ought to love their wives as their own bodies. He who loves his wife loves himself. After all, no one ever hated their own body, but they feed and care for their body, just as Christ does the church— for we are members of his body. "For this reason a man will leave his father and mother and be united to his wife, and the two will become one flesh." This is a profound mystery—but I am talking about Christ and the church. However, each one of you also must love his wife as he loves himself, and the wife must respect her husband.

Ephesians 5:22-33

Husbands, likewise, dwell with them with understanding, giving honor to the wife, as to the weaker vessel, and as being heirs together of the grace of life, that your prayers may not be hindered.

1 Peter 3:7

So many women get caught up in these verses, thinking that God must love men more, but you couldn't be farther from the truth. This verse in Galatians explicitly states that we are all equally loved in God's eyes. We have to stop going by the world's ideology of things, and start focusing on God's. Yes, God has an order of things, but this has nothing to do with God loving one more than the other. This is just how He made things to exist. Trying to change God's order of things, is like you trying to take a whale that lives in the sea, and make it live on land. It won't work, because God didn't design it that way.

Remember, He is the creator, not us.

All believers have the same redemption of sins, Jesus died for both men and women, we are all equally loved, and we all get to be with God one day. Focus on this, not the world's viewpoint.

And remember, God does not love men more than women, we are all equally loved.

Galatians 4:1-7

If someone is born with an inheritance, he does not receive his inheritance, until the Father has set the time for him to receive it. Therefore, those who were under the law, were under the law until the time that God had preordained. When the fullness of the time had come, God sent forth His Son, and redeemed those who were under the law, that we may receive adoption as His children. He did this so that those who believe in Jesus's name, would become true children of God. And for those of us who believe in our Lord Jesus's death and resurrection, we were given the promised Holy Spirit.

Therefore, we are no longer enemies of God, but heirs of God through Jesus Christ. If we were still bound to the law, we would still be slaves to sin. Jesus took on our sins, and canceled the debt that we owed.

Once you were alienated from God and were enemies in your minds because of your evil behavior. But now he has reconciled you by Christ's physical body through death to present you holy in his sight, without blemish and free from accusation— if you continue in your faith, established and firm, and do not move from the hope held out in the gospel. This is the gospel that you heard and that has been proclaimed to every creature under heaven, and of which I, Paul, have become a servant.

Colossians 1:21-23

For if, while we were God's enemies, we were reconciled to him through the death of his Son, how much more, having been reconciled, shall we be saved through his life!

Romans 5:10

When you were dead in your sins and in the uncircumcision of your flesh, God made you alive with Christ. He forgave us all our sins, having canceled the charge of our legal indebtedness, which stood against us and condemned us; he has taken it away, nailing it to the cross. And having disarmed the powers and authorities, he made a public spectacle of them, triumphing over them by the cross.

Colossians 2:13-15

Just because we are not under the law, but under grace, does not mean that we shouldn't follow what His word says, because once we follow Christ, we will want to follow the law. What this means however, is that we are no longer under law, but grace through Jesus Christ, as I explained previously.

Galatians 4:8-11

Before, they served gods who were not the true God. Now, even though they serve the one true God, they are straying in their ways, in ways that don't fit who they are in Christ. They are going back to the things which they were previously in bondage from. Paul is afraid for them, unless he had labored for them in vain.

Galatians 4:14-16

Paul faced a trial, which was in his flesh. He battled against his flesh, and as he battled, they did not reject or despise him. They received him just as they would receive an angel of God or Christ Jesus. At one point, they would have given him their own eyes, but now, because he speaks the truth, are they now his enemy?

Galatians 4:17-18

It is good to put your time and effort into things that you believe in, if the purpose is good. But, some people try to make you stray from this, leading you to put your time, support, and effort into things that are not good. These people try to make you stray from what is good and pleasing to the Lord.

This is why it is a good thing, to make sure that the friends you keep, are the ones that God has placed in your life. It is wise to pray to God, and ask Him to reveal to you anyone, or anything that is in your life, that shouldn't be. Also ask Him for the strength to remove the things that don't belong. He will help you.

Fear not, for I am with you;
Be not dismayed, for I am your God.
I will strengthen you,
Yes, I will help you,
I will uphold you with My righteous right hand.'

Isaiah 41:10

Galatians 4:21-31

These people wanted to be under the law, but this is not how things were meant to be, not to the free anyway. There are two types of people. There are ones born free, who are children of Sarah, and there are ones born of bondage, who are children of Hagar, that is, the flesh. Hagar's son was born from a fleshly desire, and Sarah's son, was born of the promise of God. As the bondwoman was cast out, so will the children of this world, the ones born to perdition. Believers are not children of this world, not children of the bondwoman, but children of the free (Sarah).

Galatians 5:1

We must stand firm, firmly fixing our eyes on Jesus, by which we have freedom in His name. Do not again be entangled together with the bondage that you were once in.

Before you believed, you were in bondage, as the child of Hagar. Now, because you believe, you have become free, as a child born of Sarah. What once entangled you was cut off, and you had broken free from this bondage. And when the Son sets you free, you are free indeed. If you are free, which you are, then why would you allow yourself to be entangled once again, with what Christ already defeated in you? You are already free, so do not become entangled yet again, with what you were already set free of.

If you allow yourself to become entangled again, it is equivalent to a person being trapped in barb wire, God coming and setting them free, and then that person going right back into the barb wire. Why inflict the pain on yourself, when you were already set free from it?

If you are allowing that bondage to entrap you again, then you have to ask God to help you remove it, because only He knows how. Whether it's guilt, shame, your past, your present, your future, your childhood, your marriage, addiction, divorce, or whatever else it is that may be keeping you in bondage, you have to lay it down.

If you feel ashamed or full of guilt, then I have a message that I want to share with you. Please read this with your whole heart.

YOU ARE FORGIVEN, AND YOU ARE SET FREE!

You have to realize that Jesus already defeated all of your guilt, shame, etc, at the cross. Why are you trying to pay twice, for a debt already paid? Would you double pay off your mortgage, a credit card, or a car? Of course not! It would be foolish and a waste of your time, effort, and resources. So why are you doing it now? Jesus paid the debt already. All is already forgiven, and your slate has already been wiped clean. Sometimes one of the hardest things for us to forgive, is ourselves. God forgave you, so why can't you forgive you?

Whether it's a bad childhood, a broken marriage, an addiction, or whatever it may be, you have to move forward. You can't move forward, if you are always looking back. If I am driving a car, and my eyes are behind me, how could I drive? I can't! I would eventually crash. In the same sense, you have to keep your focus on the race that is right in front of you, throwing off everything that hinders you. If you don't, then you will keep crashing.

If you are trying to take your baggage with you, then I am here to tell you that it's too heavy for you to carry, and you need to lay it down at Jesus's feet. You want so badly to move to the next chapter of your life, but God is trying to tell you, that in order to move forward, you have to leave things behind. You can't take them with you where God is leading you. You have to let them go. And God will help you do that, all you need to do is ask Him. Ask Him, and surrender.

God keeps taking the baggage from you, and you keep picking it back up again. Stop taking it back! The only one who is strong enough to carry it, is God. Give Him all of your burdens, and He will take from you those things that are hindering your race.

Cast your burden on the LORD,
And He shall sustain you;
He shall never permit the righteous to be moved.

Psalm 55:22

Come to me, all you who are weary and burdened, and I will give you rest. Take my yoke upon you and learn from me, for I am gentle and humble in heart, and you will find rest for your souls.

Matthew 11:28-29

Focus. Stay in your own lane. Don't look to the left, right, behind, around, etc. Keep running your race, and allow no one to hinder you. Remember, there will always be distractions, but that doesn't mean that you have to succumb to them. Focus on the task at hand, and run your race with perseverance. The enemy would love nothing more than for you to be distracted. Focus. Don't look at anything but what's ahead. Focus.

I want you to always remember something. If you are still breathing, then you still have time to change things. God will never give up on you, so don't give up on Him. God wants you to succeed. Trust Him to help you.

As you are waiting on God, He is waiting on you. He is waiting for you to let go. To give Him all that you have, and leave it there.

Do you ever have those moments, when you say that you just can't take anymore pain, trials, or suffering? Your holding on for dear life, and you feel yourself slipping. Your faith is slipping, the pain in your heart is growing, and you just don't know how much longer you can hold on. Sometimes, all it takes is for you to let go, in order to realize that you were never the one holding onto anything in first place. God is. He was just waiting for you to realize it.

Remember, He has already risen, and it is already finished. So be the child that God called you to be, a free one.

Galatians 5:2-6

Circumcision profits nothing. If you are becoming circumcised hoping to gain freedom, you are false in your thinking, because Christ will profit you nothing. Those who become circumcised, become a debtor to the whole law. If you do this, you are now a stranger to Christ, one who attempts to be justified by the law, and have fallen from grace. For it is only by grace, through faith, in which you are saved, not by works.

I want to point out that this does not mean that it is wrong to circumcise your child. What it does mean, is that if you are doing it to uphold the law, then it will profit you nothing. For example, if you are doing so for hygiene reasons, then this is OK. But, if you are doing so to uphold the law, then you have to come to terms with the fact that it profits you nothing. Whether circumcised or uncircumcised, neither profit anything. What does profit you, is faith, working through love.

Galatians 5:7-10

You were running well, but then you were hindered. Who hindered you in your race? The God who calls you, is not the one who persuades you to stray. When you make bread, a little yeast, works through the whole dough. In the same way, a little false truth, a little straying, and a little false teaching, works through the whole body. Therefore, be careful.

I am certain in you, in the Lord, that you will have no other mind, and that whoever has troubled you, shall bear his judgment, whoever they are.

Galatians 5:13-14

You have been called to be free, through Christ Jesus. Do not therefore use this freedom to gratify the flesh. We are not called to serve our flesh, but to serve one another with love. The law is fulfilled in one word, even in this: You shall love your neighbor as yourself. Did not Jesus die for you because of love? Love for someone other than Himself? Therefore, follow in Christ's footsteps, and love.

Galatians 5:15

If you choose to devour one another with words and anger, bitterness and wrath, beware, unless you become consumed by one another!

Galatians 5:16-18

Therefore, walk in the Spirit, and you shall not fulfill the desires of the flesh.
If you ever wonder why you try so hard to walk by the Spirit, but something inside of you attacks you into going the opposite way, this is the flesh. The flesh and the Spirit war against each other, as they have nothing in common. The flesh wants the things of this world, and the Spirit wants the things of God. It is a war that will persist while we live on this earth, but take heart, for one day we will live with Christ, and when we do, this will not be an issue.

While we are on this earth, we must persistently war in the fight against the flesh, however, if we keep walking in the Spirit, our flesh will die more and more, and it will become easier and easier to walk in the Spirit. You have to remember that the Spirit controls the flesh, not the other way around. If you don't believe in Jesus, then this is not the same for you, but if you do believe, and are a child of God, then this holds true. The Spirit of promise that is inside of you, has all power and dominion over the flesh, because He is God, and He rules over all. However, if you don't have Jesus, then you don't have the Spirit of promise. You must believe that Jesus is Lord, you must believe that Jesus died, and you must believe that God raised Him from the dead. Only then, can you be saved.

Galatians 5:19-21

You will know the works of the flesh, by seeing their fruits. The fruits of the flesh, are not like the fruits of the Spirit.

If you choose to live by the flesh, then you have no inheritance in the kingdom of God. Therefore, walk by the Spirit, and do not gratify the desires of the flesh.

Galatians 5:22-25

These are the fruits of the Spirit. We live by the Spirit, we walk by the Spirit, and we bear the fruits of the Spirit.

Those who choose to live for Christ, and those who are Christ's, have chosen to carry their crosses and follow Jesus. This means that the flesh, and its worldly passions and desires, are dead, and we no longer walk by them. We are now a new creation in Christ, and as such, we walk by the Spirit.

Remember, we do not produce the fruits of the Spirit, we bear them. This means that it is not our job to produce the fruit, but to abide in Christ, as He abides in us. And as we do this, we begin to bear more and more of His fruit.

"I am the true vine, and My Father is the vinedresser. Every branch in Me that does not bear fruit He takes away; and every branch that bears fruit He prunes, that it may bear more fruit. You are already clean because of the word which I have spoken to you. Abide in Me, and I in you. As the branch cannot bear fruit of itself, unless it abides in the vine, neither can you, unless you abide in Me.

"I am the vine, you are the branches. He who abides in Me, and I in him, bears much fruit; for without Me you can do nothing.

John 15:1-5

Galatians 5:26

Do not become conceited, boasting in one's self, instead, boast in Christ. Do not deliberately provoke someone to anger, wrath, resentment, bitterness, etc. Instead, with a humble heart, love others as yourself. Do not want for what others have, but be happy with what you have in Christ Jesus, knowing that He has given you everything that you need, and that what you need, can only be found in Him.

Galatians 6:1-2

If someone has sinned, do not berate or belittle them, but show gentleness. Also, guard yourself, lest you be tempted as well. Bear one another's burdens. Give a listening ear, pray for them, and be attentive to their cries for help. Bear their burdens, and so fulfill the law of Christ.

Galatians 6:6

When you yourself are taught something in the word, you should be bold to share that truth with the one who teaches.

We can always increase in learning, so sharing the truth that you have learned, helps others grow in Christ as well. And those who are wise, listen.

A wise man will hear and increase learning,
And a man of understanding will attain wise counsel,
To understand a proverb and an enigma,
The words of the wise and their riddles.
The fear of the LORD is the beginning of knowledge,
But fools despise wisdom and instruction.

Proverbs 1:5-7

Galatians 6:7

Do not be deceived into thinking that whatever you sow, you will not also reap. God is just, and whatever a man sows, this he will also reap. If you sow the things of the flesh, and the things of this world, you will reap corruption. However, if you sow the things of the Spirit, you shall reap everlasting life.

Galatians 6:9

Do not give up the hope that is within you. Do not become weary in doing good, because at just the right time, God's timing, you will reap a harvest, if you do not give up.

Take the seasons for example. In winter, flowers wither, leaves have fallen, trees go dormant, and all the beauty that once was, gets frozen for those moments of time. But, when the season of spring comes, it brings beauty, foliage, and fruit. How did the flowers, trees, and beauty make it to the spring? By enduring the harsh season, and coldness of winter. By knowing in their season, God will make everything beautiful, in its time. The same holds true for us. We anticipate the end of winter, knowing that the seasons will change, and God will make all things beautiful again, in His time. Wait for it, it will come.

Galatians 6:10

Therefore, whenever we have the opportunity, let us do good to all, especially to those who are children of God.

Galatians 6:14-17

Do not boast in anything but the cross of our Lord and Savior Christ Jesus, by whom you have died to this world and the world to you. You are no longer of the world, but of Christ. We are but foreigners here on earth, waiting for the arrival of our God and Savior.

Those who are in Christ Jesus, circumcision means nothing, for we are a new creation in Christ.

Whoever walks according to this, may peace and mercy be upon them.

We died with Him, let us also live with Him.

Galatians 6:18

Brethren, the grace of our Lord Jesus Christ be with your spirit, Amen.

See the next page for a bonus!

<u>Bonus page</u>

You can not have eternal life, without the Son, you can not be saved, without the Son, and you can not overcome the world, without the Son. I can not stress enough, that you need Jesus in order for any of this to work. Please read the scripture below for more clarity. Before you read it, please pray to God and ask for clarity, discernment, and that your eyes may be opened to the truth.

Everyone who believes that Jesus is the Christ is born of God, and everyone who loves the father loves his child as well. This is how we know that we love the children of God: by loving God and carrying out his commands. In fact, this is love for God: to keep his commands. And his commands are not burdensome, for everyone born of God overcomes the world. This is the victory that has overcome the world, even our faith. Who is it that overcomes the world? Only the one who believes that Jesus is the Son of God.

This is the one who came by water and blood—Jesus Christ. He did not come by water only, but by water and blood. And it is the Spirit who testifies, because the Spirit is the truth. For there are three that testify: the Spirit, the water and the blood; and the three are in agreement. We accept human testimony, but God's testimony is greater because it is the testimony of God, which he has given about his Son. Whoever believes in the Son of God accepts this testimony. Whoever does not believe God has made him out to be a liar, because they have not believed the testimony God has given about his Son. And this is the testimony: God has given us eternal life, and this life is in his Son. Whoever has the Son has life; whoever does not have the Son of God does not have life.

I write these things to you who believe in the name of the Son of God so that you may know that you have eternal life.

1 John 5:1-13

If you have never accepted Jesus in your life before, I am here to help you along the way. The bible tells us in Romans 10:9, *that if you confess with your mouth the Lord Jesus and believe in your heart that God has raised Him from the dead, you will be saved.*

If you are ready to accept Jesus, here is a prayer to help guide you.

Dear God,

I come to You today, recognizing that I am a sinner and in need of Your saving grace. I confess with my mouth that Jesus is Lord, and I believe that He died and You raised Him from the dead. You did this to save me. Thank You Jesus for loving me so much, that You gave your life to save mine. From here on out, I want to live my life for You, and only You. Help me live a life that pleases You. Thank You for all You have done for me. In Jesus name I pray, Amen.

If you prayed that prayer, I am so proud of you! The bible tells us that as soon as we accept Jesus, we are given the promised Holy Spirit. You now have the only One who can help you overcome this world, God Himself.

The journey may not be easy, but I promise you, it's worth it. The temporary trials of this life, could never outweigh the eternity that you will get to spend with a loving God, who calls you His child.

Welcome to our family.

To see more books by Tentmaker Ministries, please go to Tm-ministries.com

www.ingramcontent.com/pod-product-compliance
Lightning Source LLC
Chambersburg PA
CBHW010220140626
46545CB00013B/3055